First Principles:
TOPICAL STUDIES FOR NEW CONVERTS

by

Gary **and Marylyn** Underwood

For Granville Jones
who taught us both

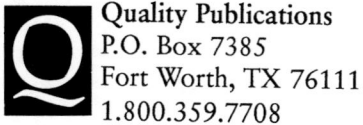

Quality Publications
P.O. Box 7385
Fort Worth, TX 76111
1.800.359.7708

© Gary and Marylyn Underwood 1978

All rights reserved. No part of this publication may be reproduced, stored in a retrieval system, or transmitted in any form or by any means electronic, mechanical, photo copy, recording, or otherwise, without prior permission of the copyright owner.

ISBN 0-89137-709-3

TABLE OF CONTENTS

INTRODUCTION 2

LESSON I: THE LORD'S SUPPER 5

LESSON II: PRAYER 9

LESSON III: THE ORIGIN OF THE CHURCH 13

LESSON IV: THE ORGANIZATION OF THE CHURCH. 17

LESSON V: THE AUTHORITY OF THE CHURCH. 21

LESSON VI: THE MISSION AND GREATNESS OF THE CHURCH 25

LESSON VII: SALVATION AND CHURCH MEMBERSHIP. 29

LESSON VIII: HOW TO BECOME A MEMBER 33

LESSON IX: MEMBERSHIP, ITS RESPONSIBILITIES 37

LESSON X: OUR STEWARDSHIP 41

LESSON XI: FORSAKING THE ASSEMBLY 47

LESSON XII: EVANGELISTS 51

LESSON XIII: DEACONS. 55

LESSON XIV: ELDERS 55

LESSON XV: PERSONAL TEACHING 61

LESSON XVI: MUSIC IN THE WORSHIP. 66

LESSON XVII: THE MARRIAGE RELATIONSHIP 71

INTRODUCTION

The topical outlines in this booklet, original author(s) unknown, have been revised and enlarged by the present authors for the specific purpose of better instructing new converts. This material has been successfully taught to new converts over a period of fifteen years, and, where the new members have stayed with the program, has proven a deciding factor in their continuing service to the Lord. The outline is a list of Scriptures, God's Word, on a particular topic with virtually no editorial comment on the Scriptures. Introductory and/or concluding paragraphs serve simply as a preface to or a summary for the lesson. This, I am convinced, is one reason for the topical studies' success. However, prior to each topical lesson are some additional comments based on what questions have been raised by converts we have taught and on some observations made by my wife and me in the teaching/learning/studying situation.

We, as a team, decided initially that new converts needed more than a film series of six weeks' duration or a classroom setting where the shy, new Christian might feel somewhat intimidated by older converts or by older members who are just "sitting in" to relearn first principles. Too, these classes (usually meeting on Wednesday night or on Sunday morning) often do not materialize because of a lack of numbers. To some in authority it seems easier to put the new convert in a regular classroom because of (1) lack of space, or (2) lack of a willing teacher, or (3) lack of understanding for the new convert's needs. If such a class is set up at one of these times, however, it is a recognition of the latter half of the Great Commission: ". . .teaching them always to observe all things whatsoever I have commanded you." Obviously, any class specifically set aside for new converts is better than no class. But we have found that even better than this is an informal class in the convert's own home with my wife and me working together as a team. This "team teaching" (using the phrase loosely) has multiple advantages, but to name a few:

1. It puts the couple more at ease.

2. It causes more discussion by injection of more than one point of view.

3. It makes for the perception of two people rather than one, as the wife member of the team may see that a particular point is hazy or belabored, or vice versa.

4. Since the two members of the team act as a stimulant, or catalyst, one to the other, it is conducive to energetic, lively teaching.

The present study is introduced to the new convert **upon his conversion**, and it is taught in the convert's home. To do this means scheduling the class at the new Christian's convenience, not your own. There are, with all programs of this type, problems that cannot be foreseen; but the advantages, once the class is underway, far outweigh any problems one might encounter in initially establishing the class. For instance, I recall one situation where the new convert's husband was adamant about not being present for any of the study sessions even though he was a "member," but after a month of first one excuse, then another, he started appearing for the sessions, getting home "in time" for a pleasant change. Now he and his wife both are willing workers for the Lord. Two souls were saved, not one. We could not afford to say, "Well, since he won't come, let's not teach her," or "Maybe we ought to wait until he is more receptive to this program." We had to be willing to adjust.

Another initial adjustment—the hardest for many—is a commitment to at least an eighteen-week program. We say **at least** because more often than not, the convert (and his/her mate who is also involved in the study) becomes so interested in a particular topical lesson that one session simply won't suffice. We have, for example, spent three weeks on **one** lesson. One thing the teacher must understand from the beginning of the class: he is committing himself to about five months in seeing the new convert's interest in God's Word increase and in his becoming more mature in understanding. Five months is a small price to pay to study the Bible with someone zealous to learn.

In setting up the class, it is best to ask the convert upon his baptism when he/she is most open to a study and before he/she becomes too "settled" in his new religious surroundings. Most converts are affable, eager to learn and immediately agree to a home Bible class. When the class does finally meet, it is best to study around the kitchen or dining room table so that Bibles and Bible helps are accessible for easy reference and also because it provides a casual atmosphere with incentive for open participation. Scriptures are read by each participant in a round-the-table fashion, each student taking his turn reading a Scripture and making comment. Of course, you as the teacher, will make additional comments. But the Socratic method of question and answer still works and makes one think. Discussion must be open; views must be allowed to be expressed. However, truth must be taught. You are in charge. Be dominant, but not domineering, remembering always that it is the Word that teaches. The new convert is anxious to learn, so he will allow you expression with a great deal of interest and concern.

It is important, though, that you recognize his individual problems coming from the denominational world; therefore, you need to be aware of the major teachings of the convert's past religious questions. Many times a question has been asked and the "pat" answer did not fill the person's need. For example, once, when teaching a Catholic, a Christian friend simply could not answer to the Catholic's satisfaction any number of queries because of a lack of communication. Knowing that I had once been affiliated with Catholicism and therefore acquainted with the doctrines of that body, the brother called on me to approach the problem. My insights enabled me to provide answers to questions that were not asked, but were implied. The result of that study was the baptism of that individual.

In addition to the program's success being based on the material itself—God's Word regarding particular subjects—and on the establishment of an at-home study, this program, finally, has proven effective because the new Christian needs fellowship. The five months spent with a couple (the new convert and his/her wife/husband) around their table make for a lasting friendship and a loving relationship. This time is wisely spent and cannot help being beneficial to teacher and student alike. From such classes we have heard comments from mates who were already members, such as, "I wondered why we (the church) did that," or "I've never really **studied** the Bible before now." For my wife and me, the tightly focused studies have done more than mere words can express. And though we have gone over the same material for fifteen years, the questions asked by new members with varying denominational/religious backgrounds always make the classes interesting, varied, informative, and most of all, challenging.

We wish you, the teacher, God's blessing in your teaching this class. We wish you, the new convert, the happiness that comes from a study of God's Word and the understanding that is based on faith and a loving desire to penetrate ever deeper into the most exciting of books, the Bible.

Gary M. Underwood

An outline is only
as warm
as the person presenting it.

LESSON I: THE LORD'S SUPPER

Because the new Christian's first observance of the Lord's Supper has special significance to him, he wants to know—and needs to know—**why** he is partaking of it. It is his first active participation of worship as a new Christian. Therefore, this topic is studied first. The convert needs to understand that this is not a ritual, but a memorial. He also needs to be enlightened as to the consequences should he partake of it unworthily. The questions at the end of this study are some most frequently asked.

THE LORD'S SUPPER

Scriptural Text:
Matthew 26:26-28; Mark 14:22-24; Luke 22:19, 20; 1 Corinthians 11:17-34

Introduction: The fact that so many people believe and practice so many things about the Lord's Supper shows that there are misunderstandings about it. Jehovah has spoken concerning the Lord's Supper and we must be guided by what He has said.

What is the Lord's Supper?

A. It is a memorial (something done in memory of someone) 1 Corinthians 11:23-26.

   1. A memorial that preaches Christ's death. 1 Corinthians 11:26

   2. It preaches His second coming. 1 Corinthians 11:26

   3. It preaches the new covenant. 1 Corinthians 11:25; Matthew 26:28

How often to observe?

A. It is God, and not the church, who regulates this.

   1. The Jerusalem church continued steadfastly. Acts 2:42

   2. The Troas church. Acts 20:7 (Note: the first day of the week—Sunday—is not the Sabbath.)
   3. The church at Corinth. 1 Corinthians 11:18; 16:1, 2

Who shall take part in the Lord's Supper?

A. We can learn who should by learning who did.

   1. Members of the Jerusalem church. Acts 2:42

   2. Members of the Troas church. Acts 20:7

   3. Members of the church at Corinth. 1 Corinthians 11:28-33

   4. Those in the kingdom. Luke 22:29, 30

5. It is a communion of the individual and the Lord. 1 Corinthians 10:16

Some Questions

A. Will taking the Lord's Supper too often destroy its meaning?

B. What is it to eat and drink "unworthily"? 1 Corinthians 11:27

C. What is the meaning of the "cup"? 1 Corinthians 11:25

D. Is the bread turned into the Lord's literal (real) body, and the fruit of the vine into His literal blood? John 6:54, 63

E. Is the Lord's Supper necessary? Must the Christian eat and drink at the Lord's Table? 1 Corinthians 11:24-29; John 6:51-58

LESSON II: PRAYER

The new Christian has established a brand new relationship with his God. To cultivate this new love, prayer as a topic for study is most important. New members of Christ's body, especially the men, are especially anxious to learn about public praying. I have, in our own classes, told the following true happening: shortly after my own conversion, I was called upon from the pulpit to lead a closing prayer without prior notice. I began falteringly but became so involved in my prayer with the almighty God, that I choked up and could not finish. After an embarrassing silence, a beautiful brother near me finished the prayer. This true story I tell to illustrate the love and patience of the brethren.

The new member would do well to pray before each study session in order to become accustomed to hearing his own voice in public prayer.

PRAYER

Scriptural Text:
1 Thessalonians 5:17-19

Introduction: One of the outstanding duties, privileges and joys of the Christian is prayer. It is the Father's will and desire that His children pray. What a privilege to "come boldly unto the throne of grace, that we may obtain mercy, and find grace to help in time of need" (Hebrews 4:16). It gives joy to know that "the effectual fervent prayer of a righteous man availeth much" (James 5:16).

Christ prayed much.

A. He left us an example. 1 Peter 2:21

B. Some examples of His praying:

   1. Beginning of His ministry. Luke 3:21

   2. Before the twelve were selected. Luke 6:12

   3. After teaching the multitudes. Matthew 14:23

   4. In the early morning. Mark 1:35

   5. In the Garden before His crucifixion. Matthew 26:36-42; John 17

The early church was strong in prayer.

A. The three thousand. Acts 2:41, 42

B. When Peter was imprisoned. Acts 12:5

C. The churches admonished to pray.

   1. Rome. Romans 12:12

   2. Corinth. 1 Corinthians 7:5

   3. Ephesus. Ephesians 6:18

   4. Philippi. Philippians 4:6, 7

God's promise to answer prayer is conditional.

A. Be righteous. 1 Peter 3:12

B. Be obedient. 1 John 3:22-24; John 9:31

C. Pray in faith. Matthew 21:22; James 1:6, 7

D. Have forgiving spirit. Matthew 6:15

E. Abide in Christ. John 15:7

F. Have right motive. James 4:3-6

G. Pray in harmony with God's will. 1 John 5:14

H. Pray in Jesus' name. John 14:13, 14; Colossians 3:17; John 14:6 Ephesians 2:18; 1 Peter 2:5; John 5:23; Luke 10:16

Things for which to pray:

A. Forgiveness of saints' sins. 1 Thessalonians 5:25; Matthew 6:12; Acts 8:22-24

B. For help in time of temptation. Matthew 6:13; 26:41

C. For daily needs. Matthew 6:11

D. For rulers. 1 Timothy 2:1, 2

E. For the sick. James 5:14

F. For enemies. Matthew 5:44

G. For laborers to enter the harvest. Matthew 9:38

H. For preachers, and for the Lord's word to be glorified. 2 Thessalonians 3:1

I. For God's children. Philippians 1:9-11

J. For God's will to be done. Matthew 6:10; 26:39

Conclusion: Prayer is not only the expression of gratitude and need but is a high and beautiful expression of trust, submission and union with God. Let us pray so as to be understood by others when praying publicly. 1 Corinthians 14:4, 9, 16

LESSON III: THE ORIGIN OF THE CHURCH

Probably this study is already fairly well understood, since the establishment of the church at Pentecost is a prominent part of most cottage classes. It puts in proper perspective the place of the true kingdom. Most new converts, therefore, having studied this topic before, feel free to comment and enjoy the lesson. It is important to note that, contrary to Catholic dogma, the church of Christ was the first church established; indeed, it is the only church because Christ died for His church. The schisms created by denominations would be non-existent if the religious world could discern this fact.

THE ORIGIN OF THE CHURCH

Scriptural Text:
Matthew 16:16-18; Acts 2:31-41

Introduction: It is important to know when the church began for at least two reasons: (1) a matter of identity—to distinguish it from Old Testament agencies and also from religious institutions of human origin; and (2) to identify its laws—to see when the law governing the church of God went into effect.

Church foreshadowed in Old Testament. Hebrews 9:11, 23; 10:1

A. The church was not in existence in Old Testament days. (Last days, New Testament. Hebrews 1:1, 2)

B. Old Testament worthies desired to see its era. 1 Peter 1:10-12

Church not established by John.

A. Preached "at hand," or approaching. Matthew 3:1, 2, 11; John 1:19, 20, 23

B. John was not in the kingdom. Matthew 11:11

Church not established during personal ministry of Jesus.

A. Time of waiting over—"at hand." Mark 1:15

B. "At hand." Matthew 10:7

C. "Come nigh unto you." Luke 10:9

D. Disciples taught to pray for it. Matthew 6:9, 10

E. Christ promised to build it. Matthew 16:18 (Later—after it is built—1 Corinthians 3:10; Ephesians 2:20-22)

F. Disciples not yet in it. Matthew 18:1-3

G. Christ's promise that it will come during that generation. Mark 9:1

H. Disciples yet expecting. Luke 22:18; 19:11; Mark 15:43

I. Had not come at time of ascension. Acts 1:6-8

The beginning.

A. Kingdom to begin and law to go forth from Jerusalem. Acts 1:8; Isaiah 2:2, 3; Luke 24:47

B. Law went forth from Jerusalem on Pentecost. Acts 2:37-39

C. Pentecost the beginning. Acts 2:1-4; 11:15

D. The kingdom to come with power. Mark 9:1

E. The power to come with Holy Spirit. Acts 1:8

F. The Holy Spirit on Pentecost. Acts 2:1-4

G. Apostles commissioned to preach. Matthew 28:18-20; Mark 16:15, 16

H. Apostles instructed to wait in Jerusalem for Holy Spirit. Luke 24:49

I. Spirit came on Pentecost; preaching of the gospel, the law of the kingdom, began on Pentecost. Acts 2:31-38

Pentecost marks the beginning. Acts 11:15

A. Beginning of the Christian age—the New Covenant. Hebrews 7:18, 19; 8:7-9; 10:15-17.

B. Beginning of the church.

C. Beginning of gospel preaching.

D. Beginning of preaching of the remissiion of sins. Luke 24:47

After Pentecost the church or kingdom always spoken of as in existence.

Acts 2:47; 5:11; 8:1; 11:22; 13:1; 14:27; Colossians 1:13-18; Revelations 1:9

Conclusion: The church, promised and planned by God, was built by the Christ, "the Son of the Living God" (Matthew 16:16). His kingdom is everlasting, remaining to this very day. See Daniel 2:44.

LESSON IV: THE ORGANIZATION OF THE CHURCH

The new member usually is doubly curious about this topic: he wants to know more about the physical make-up of the church, and he is desirous of understanding the autonomous nature of the church. The latter is particularly appealing since there is none like it in the denominational world; and when one discovers this is God's plan, he wonders at the hierarchy in the world's "Christendom."

THE ORGANIZATION OF THE CHURCH

Scriptural Text:
Colossians 4:15; Acts 14:23

Introduction: Christ is the spiritual head of the body, and His subjects are those who follow Him (James 2:5). His word governs the church (Matthew 28:18). Its design was practiced by early Christians and is recorded in the New Testament for us.

Two uses of the word "church" in the New Testament.

A. **Universal**—comprehensive sense including all saved of the earth. Matthew 16:18; 1 Timothy 3:15; Ephesians 1:22, 23. In this sense the family of God, body of Christ, kingdom of God, are the same. Not an organization in the universal sense, it knows no authority but Christ and His word. Whoever does the will of God and obeys the Word belongs to it. Acts 2:41, 47

B. **Local**—in limited sense including all God's people in one community. 1 Corinthians 1:2; Romans 16:16; Acts 14:23; 5:11; 8:1, "in Jerusalem"; Acts 13:1; 15:22

The organization of the local church.

A. An established order: "in every church," Acts 14:23; "set in order the things that are lacking," Titus 1:5

B. An independent self-governing unit, always spoken of as separate units: ". . . churches of Galatia," Galatians 1:2; "churches of Judea," Galatians 1:22. Several independent churches in one district, but no district organization: 1 Corinthians 14:33-40. In this comprehensive injunction, given to a church, is implied control of its affairs by the church.

C. A plurality of elders in every church. Acts 14:23; 20:17

D. Deacons. Philippians 1:1. Bishops and deacons of Philippian church.

E. Members. Romans 12:4; 16:1, 2; 1 Corinthians 12:27. Identification with a local church was a practice of New Testament days.

Local organization only medium through which early Christians worked.

A. New Testament mentions no other.

B. Every good work done through local organizations. Ephesians 3:10

    1. Missions. Sent out by local church, Acts 13:1-3; reported to local church, Acts 14:25-28.

    2. Charity. Acts 11:29, 30. Funds for poor saints in Judea were placed in hands of elders of Jerusalem church to be administered by them.

Cooperation of local churches.

A. Local churches cooperated in doing their work. Romans 15:25, 26; 2 Corinthians 8:1-5

B. Such work was under the supervision of a local church and its eldership. Acts 11:28-30; Romans 15:25, 26; 1 Corinthians 16:1-3

Conclusion: Various scriptural methods may be used in carrying on the work of the local church; but other organizations, either within or without, were unknown in the first century and are therefore unscriptural now.

LESSON V: THE AUTHORITY OF THE CHURCH

Following the lesson on organization, this study states firmly that our authority is in Christ as the Son of God. It is not in man but in Jesus, the Messiah, our Savior, on whom we rely and to whom we go for all things. The emphasis is on Him and His message. After this lesson, one understands more than ever the meaning of the church as Christ's **kingdom**.

THE AUTHORITY OF THE CHURCH

Scriptural Text:
Matthew 28:18-20; Ephesians 1:20-23

Introduction: There is no man on earth, regardless of his position, who has preeminence over Christ—no prophet, no priest, no king, no government. Christ is the supreme authority.

The source of authority: God speaking through Christ.

A. Hebrews 1:1, 2—New Testament message and messenger contrasted with Old.

B. John 1:17—Moses the lawgiver in Old Testament period, Christ giver of grace and truth in the New.

C. Matthew 11:27—God revealed through Christ.

D. John 5:26, 27—Authority given to Christ.

E. John 17:6-15—Christ's message from God. John 12:48-50

We are to be governed today by the authority of Christ, not Moses and the prophets.

A. Acts 3:19-23; Mark 9:2-8—"Hear ye HIM."

B. Matthew 5:21, 22; 5:27, 28—"But I say unto you."

C. 1 Corinthians 9:21—"Under law to Christ."

Christ's authority to be executed through His apostles.

A. Matthew 19:27, 28; Matthew 28:18-20; Mark 16:17-19

B. John 20:22, 23

C. 2 Corinthians 5:18-20

D. 1 John 4:6

Apostles to be guided by Holy Spirit.

A. John 14:16, 17

B. John 14:26

C. John 16:7-15

D. Luke 24:49

E. Acts 2:1-4, 37, 38

Preaching of apostles confirmed by miracles. Mark 16:15-18, 20; Hebrews 2:1-4; 1 Corinthians 12:28-31; 1 Corinthians 12:1-11; 13:8-12. These gifts served temporary purpose of introducing and confirming New Testament truths.

Completeness of law thus delivered.

A. Romans 1:16, 17

B. 2 Peter 1:3

C. 2 Timothy 3:14-17

D. Jude 3

E. Revelations 22:18, 19

Conclusion: The New Testament Scriptures containing God's will revealed through Christ and His chosen ambassadors, guided and confirmed in their message by the Holy Spirit, constitute a complete and perfect rule of faith and practice for God's people today: the Divine Constitution of the Kingdom of God.

LESSON VI: THE MISSION AND GREATNESS OF THE CHURCH

This lesson is a natural follow-up of the previous lesson. Indeed, it is an elaboration of it. Most importantly, however, one becomes acutely aware of the necessity of being one of God's children. Re-emphasis needs to be on our being baptized into Christ, not being joined to any human institution, but to Christ's body. If this emphasis prevails, doubts and questions and accusations such as, "You mean you've **got** to be a member of this church to be saved?" will be of a secondary nature, for what is important, of course, is that Christ has added you to His church and has, therefore, provided for your salvation through His sacrifice and through His purchase of that church by His blood.

THE MISSION AND GREATNESS OF THE CHURCH

Scriptural Text:
1 Timothy 3:15; Ephesians 3:10

Introduction: The church of God does not occupy the place in the hearts of men that it should occupy until they realize that by staying outside of the church they rob themselves of life's greatest blessings and of the hope of eternal life. The church is incomparably greater than all human institutions, sectarian or fraternal.

God is its Author: it is therefore divine. Hebrews 3:4

A. It is God's temple. 1 Corinthians 3:16

B. His dwelling place. Ephesians 2:19-22

C. Must be built according to His directions. Hebrews 8:1-5; 9:11

D. Jesus the builder. Matthew 16:18-20

E. Must take heed how we build. 1 Corinthians 3:10-15; Psalms 127:1

F. God refuses to recognize any but His own. Matthew 15:13

G. To wear God's name. Ephesians 3:14-16

H. It is God's institution. 1 Corinthians 1:2

Christ is its Savior and Head.

A. Gave Himself for it. Ephesians 5:22-32

B. Savior of the Body. Ephesians 5:23

C. Head of the Body, which is the church. Colossians 1:18; Ephesians 1:22, 23

D. Christ our representative in Heaven. Hebrews 10:19-22; 1 John 2:1, 2

Glorious in its mission.

A. Saving souls by preaching the gospel is its design. Romans 1:16

B. The pillar and ground of the truth. 1 Timothy 3:14, 15

C. The sending agency. Romans 10:11-15; Acts 13:1-3

D. Wisdom of God made known through the church. Ephesians 3:10

E. God glorified in the church. Ephesians 3:21

All spiritual blessings are therein.

A. The church is the "fulness of Him that filleth all in all." Ephesians 1:23

B. All spiritual blessings are in Christ. Ephesians 1:3

C. Christ's body and the church are one. Ephesians 1:22, 23; Colossians 1:18

D. Christ and the church are inseparably united. Ephesians 5:28-32. Therefore, through the church we enjoy every spiritual blessing provided for us in Christ Jesus.

E. We are reconciled unto God in the body of Christ, which is the church. Ephesians 2:16; Colossians 1:18-20

F. We get into Christ and the church upon the same conditions and by the same process. Galatians 3:26, 27; Acts 2:41-47; 1 John 3:1

Conclusion: The church is made up of saved people. It is not a "tabernacle made with hands" (Hebrews 9:11), for Christ's body is the dwelling place for all who do His will. The mission of these followers of Christ is to seek others who would also submit to Him, becoming members of His church glorifying God.

LESSON VII: SALVATION AND CHURCH MEMBERSHIP

Surely it is a hard truth to realize that some are outside Christ. We must go to the Holy Scriptures for our assurance that God is merciful; He is also just. Not everyone will be saved. As members of His body, if we remain faithful, our names are and will be in the Book of Life. Our membership is conditional in our acceptance of Christ as our Savior. If we will not admit that and do not obey Him, we are none of His.

SALVATION AND CHURCH MEMBERSHIP

Scriptural Text:
Romans 6:3; Hebrews 12:23

Introduction: God does the saving. Salvation is the pardon or forgiveness of God, the "blotting out" of our sins. The church, then, does not save. The question is, "Can one enjoy the salvation that God has provided without being in the church of God?"

The essentiality and importance of the church is seen in Christ's attitude towards it.

A. Acts 20:28; 1 Peter 1:18, 19

B. Ephesians 5:25

C. Thus Christ evidenced His attitude toward the essentiality of the church by the price He paid for its existence.

D. Philippians 2:5

One cannot be "in Christ" without being "in the church."

A. Christ is the Head; the church is His body; Christians are members. Colossians 1:18; Ephesians 1:22, 23; 1 Corinthians 12:27
One cannot be joined to the head without being a member of the body which is the church.
B. Christ is the Bridegroom, the church His bride. Ephesians 5:23-32. The two are one; one cannot be related to the Christ, therefore, without being equally related to the church. A child belongs by the same birth to both the family of his father and mother.

C. To be in Christ is to be in His body, which is the church. Romans 6:3

D. To be in Christ is to be in His body, which is the chruch. Romans 6:3

   1. In Christ Jesus, made nigh, by blood. Ephesians 2:13

   2. In one body, reconciled, by the cross. Ephesians 2:17-22

3. To be in Christ, therefore, is to be in His body, and to be in His body is to be in His church.

All spiritual blessings.

A. Are in Christ Jesus. Ephesians 1:3

B. Church is the "fulness of Him that filleth all in all." Ephesians 1:23

As a member of the church.

A. To have your name enrolled in heaven. Hebrews 12:22, 23; Revelations 22:12-15

B. To not have your name enrolled in heaven means to be eternally lost at the judgment. Revelations 20:15

The same process and conditions that save from sin, makes one a Christian AND ADDS ONE TO THE CHURCH.

A. Faith, baptism, salvation. Mark 16:15, 16

B. Faith, baptism, puts one into Christ. Galatians 3:26, 27

C. Faith, baptism, adds one to the church. Acts 2:41

Conclusion: There is no such thing taught as being saved by one process and then joining the church by another. Christ said, "I am the vine, ye are the branches: He that abideth in me, and I in him, the same bringeth forth much fruit: for without me ye can do nothing" (John 15:5).

LESSON VIII: HOW TO BECOME A MEMBER

If membership is so essential, then "How to become a member" is a necessary topic for study. Though the new Christian is already aware of "how," it is good at this point in the series to re-evaluate that conversion, especially in light of the lesson on "Salvation and Church Membership." Emphasis here must center on what is taught in the Scriptures and not on what man says.

HOW TO BECOME A MEMBER

Scriptural Text:
John 3:3-6; Acts 2:37-41

Introduction: The Bible is explicit in its instructions on the subject of becoming one in Christ or becoming a member of His church. Despite this, there is much confusion in the religious world concerning membership in the Lord's body. The importance of the subject is obvious and warrants our closest study.

The testimony of Christ.

A. Must be born again. John 3:3-5

B. Must be converted. Matthew 18:1-3

C. The Great Commission. Mark 16:15, 16; Matthew 28:18-20; Luke 24:44-49

Testimony of the Apostles.

A. Saved by foolishness of preaching. 1 Corinthians 1:21

B. Must hear in order to believe. Romans 10:14-17

C. Must believe or die in sin. John 8:24; Mark 16:16

D. Must repent and be converted. Acts 3:19; Luke 13:3, 5

E. By faith baptized into Christ. Galatians 3:26, 27

F. Purify souls by obedience to doctrine. 1 Peter 1:22; 2 Timothy 3:16; John 17:17

G. Made free from sin by obedience to doctrine. Romans 6:17, 18

H. Must be led by Spirit. Romans 8:14

I. Must be washed, justified, sanctified. 1 Corinthians 6:9, 11; 1:2

Taught by figures.

A. The new birth. John 3:1-16

    1. Begotten. 1 Peter 1:23, 24; James 1:18; 1 Corinthians 4:15

    2. Born of water and Spirit. John 3:5; Galatians 3:26, 27; Acts 2:38-41

    3. Born anew. John 3:3; 1 Peter 1:3, 4

B. Marriage to Christ. Ephesians 5:23-30; Romans 7:4

    1. Acquaintanceship. John 6:44, 45

    2. Love. 1 John 4:19

    3. Ceremony. Galatians 3:26, 27

Exemplified

A. Pentecostians. Acts 2

    1. What they heard: death, burial, resurrection, and exaltation of Christ. Acts 2:22-34

    2. What they were told to do: believe beyond a doubt, repent, and be baptized in the name of Christ. Acts 2:36-38

    3. What they did: gladly received the word and were baptized. Acts 2:41

    4. Its consequences: remission of sins and gift of Holy Spirit. Acts 2:38 Added to the church. Acts 2:41, 47

B. Samaritans. Acts 8:12

C. Corinthians. Acts 18:8

D. Every conversion in the book of Acts is but a repetition of this same story. The sequence was: hearing, believing, repenting, confessing faith in Christ, and being baptized into Christ.

Conclusion: When men obey the will of God, their sins are pardoned and God recognizes and accepts them as His own children. They are added to the body of the saved and enjoy the privileges and share the responsibilities of that relationship.

LESSON IX: MEMBERSHIP, ITS RESPONSIBILITIES

Once one has become a member, then what? The new convert, as a result of this study, becomes somewhat aware of what is expected of him personally—by other church members and by God. His first allegiance is to Christ; the church is Christ's body; consequently, all responsibilities to the local congregation could be regarded as responsibilities to a part of Christ's body. One should identify himself with a local congregation so that he can better put his talents to work for the Lord. He must needs also submit himself to an eldership. Furthermore, he must realize the necessity for maintaining the precious unity of the church and his responsibility in helping to preserve that unity. I tell those with whom I study that my Christian brethren are closer to me than my own kin. Because of my Lord—and theirs—we have a closer blood relationship than even the closest family can have. We must care for each other. Finally, we, because of our love which cannot be held in, want to share with others the Gospel message.

MEMBERSHIP, ITS RESPONSIBILITIES

Scriptural Text:
Titus 3:1, 2: Romans 7:4; Galatians 6:9, 10; Philippians 1:27

Introduction: Every relationship in life that is worthwhile involves responsibilities. Membership in the church of God bestows upon one the highest and holiest privileges and blessings and, therefore, involves the greatest responsibility and most serious obligations. Some of these responsibilities are included in this study.

Local church membership.

A. Paul in his work always associated himself with a congregation of Christians. Acts 9:26-30; 13:1-3; 14:25-28

B. Since the congregation is the only unit of organization known in the New Testament for carrying forward the work of the church, it follows that for a Christian to be in full fellowship with the church, he must be associated with, be a part of and amenable to a local church.

Subjection to elders as a member of a congregation.

A. Elders to exercise oversight. 1 Peter 5:1-5

B. "Obey them that have the rule over you, and submit yourselves: for they watch for your souls . . . ." Hebrews 13:17; 1 Timothy 5:17-19

Joint participation or fellowship in the work of the local church.

A. Ready unto every good work. Titus 3:1, 2

B. Every joint supplieth. Ephesians 4:16

C. Let each man do. 1 Corinthians 9:17; 2 Corinthians 8:11-15; Galatians 6:10

D. Prove your own work. Galatians 6:4, 5

Preservation of unity, peace and harmony of the body.

A. No divisions among you. 1 Corinthians 1:10

B. No schism, same care one for another. 1 Corinthians 12:24, 25

C. Avoid them that cause division among you. Romans 16:17, 18; 1 Timothy 6:3, 4; Titus 1:10, 11; 2 John 9-11

D. Endeavor to keep unity of Spirit in bond of peace. Ephesians 4:1-3

Preservation and maintenance of the purity of the church.

A. Christ **died** to establish its purity. Ephesians 5:25-27

B. We must **live** to maintain it. 2 Timothy 2:19-22; 1 Timothy 6:11, 12; 1 Timothy 4:12; 1 Timothy 5:22; Philippians 1:27

Fruit to be borne: Church has a mission to fill, souls to save.

A. United with Christ that we might bring forth fruit unto God. Romans 7:4

B. Branches that do not bring forth fruit will be cut off. John 15:2

C. So shall ye be my disciples. John 15:8

Conclusion: A Christian should be ready always to do good; his life must be above reproach; and he should strive daily to follow the Master's Great Commission to lead others to Christ. To not do these commands is to be cut off from God (John 15:1, 2, 6).

LESSON X: OUR STEWARDSHIP

This study, because of its length, generally takes two or three sessions. It deals with something close to most of us if we are honest—our pocketbooks. A restricted responsibility, it follows rather logically the more general study of the responsibilities of a member. There is much stated in the New Testament on giving. Ordinarily, when the topic is brought up, older members feel somewhat uncomfortable. The principle of giving should be taught at the time when one has just given himself to Christ. He has gotten himself off his hands. Would all members—old, young, new—understand this lesson, that what we "have" is His, that we must give of ourselves first and the money will quite naturally follow, and that without money, the local congregation suffers with the end result of Jesus' light not shining as brightly in the community. This is not to say that one can judge a great congregation by looking at the amount of money contributed each week. But if the members could see fit to give back an ample portion of what they owe, the light **would** shine round about them.

An interesting comment has been that of disbelief and surprise when the new member discovers that whatever he chooses to give is his decision, not the preacher's nor the elders', but his alone. Nor is he told how much to give; nor will he receive letters in the mail reminding him to make up for a certain Sunday, etc., as is often done in various denominations.

OUR STEWARDSHIP

Scriptural Text:
2 Corinthians 9:6, 7

Introduction: There is more said in the Bible on stewardship than on faith, repentance, confession, baptism and the Lord's Supper all combined.

Some things to think about:

A. Everything belongs to God. Luke 16:1-15, 1 Corinthians 10:26; Acts 4:32.

B. What one owns is "his own" in relation to others. Acts 5:4. **All** belongs to God.

C. The New Testament teaches that men are God's stewards of:

    1. Their lives. Matthew 16:24-26

    2. Their abilities. Matthew 25:14-30

    3. Their time. Ephesians 5':15, 16

    4. Their money. Luke 16:1-15

D. A steward must be faithful. 1 Corinthians 4:2; 1 Peter 4:10, 11

E. Man acknowledges God's ownership by setting aside as an act of worship a definite portion of his income. 1 Corinthians 16:1-4; 2 Corinthians 9:12-15

Some principles of giving.

A. Give self first. 2 Corinthians 8:5

B. Be motivated by love. 1 Corinthians 13:3

C. Give regularly. 1 Corinthians 16:1, 2

D. Give according to one's income. 1 Corinthians 16:2

E. Consider God's part first. Matthew 6:33; James 4:15; Malachi 3:7-10

F. Give liberally. 2 Corinthians 9:6

G. Give cheerfully. 2 Corinthians 9:7

Differences in giving.

A. TIP method—no rule or purpose, but a tip is supposed to be at least one tenth.

B. ENTERTAINMENT manner—when present and if services are considered suitable.

C. SPONGE manner—under pressure.

D. TITHE method—obligatory upon the Jew.

E. CHRISTIAN method—goes beyond the tithe. Matthew 23:23; 5:20

Some blessings promised to the faithful steward.

A. Give and it shall be given unto you. Luke 6:38

B. More blessed to give than to receive. Acts 20:35

C. God is able to make all grace abound; this "Grace" refers to material blessings. 2 Corinthians 9:1-12

Why should a Christian give?

A. The obligation of being a Christian: to follow Christ is to give. Matthew 19:21; 2 Corinthians 9:13

B. The teaching of the New Testament. Matthew 6:1

C. The example of the early church. 1 Corinthians 16:1, 2

D. Obligation of a world program. Romans 15:25-27; 2 Corinthians 8:1-5

E. Obligation of a stewardship: everything belongs to God; what am I doing with the part entrusted to me? 1 John 3:17

F. Obligation of the Golden Rule. Matthew 7:12

G. Obligation of income or wealth, the means to do good to all men. Proverbs 3:27, 28; 2 Corinthians 8:14

H. Obligation of system. Romans 12:11

I. Challenge of the unfinished task: "Ye are the salt of the world. . . ." Matthew 5:13

J. Obligation to conscience. James 4:17

K. Because Christ, our example, gave **all.** Romans 5:15, John 3:16

Conclusion: Jesus asks of us all we are able to give: (1) ourselves in love; (2) our belongings freely; (3) proper use of what He has given us.

LESSON XI: FORSAKING THE ASSEMBLY

There are many new converts who are unaccustomed to meeting in worship three times a week and more often for meetings, so they are not cognizant of the importance or the necessity for their presence at every assembly. Indeed, there are older members who do not realize this fact. If we follow the early Christians' example, however, as is indicated in Acts of the Apostles, it becomes readily apparent what the Christian's responsibility here is. Not only should the Christian recognize attendance as a duty or responsibility, he should desire to attend all services—for the reasons stated in the outline, each one of which is helpful to him in remaining faithful to Christ. We are much too human; if we do not zealously and religiously seek after His Word, we will not long remain in it.

FORSAKING THE ASSEMBLY

Scriptural Text:
Hebrews 10:25

Introduction: Some do forsake the assembling together and thus forsake the teachings of God and are at fault. When we forsake a command of God, we have forsaken God.

Early Christians assembled every Lord's Day for worship.

A. Church in Jerusalem. Acts 2:42

B. Church at Troas. Acts 20:7

  1. Came together on the first day of the week for breaking the bread.

  2. Early disciples met on each first day of the week, not on the Sabbath, a Jewish custom and command. Exodus 20:8

C. Church at Corinth. 1 Corinthians 11:20; 1 Corinthians 16:2

Some other reasons for attending the services.

A. We show proof of our love for the Lord. John 14:15

B. We show our faith by our works. James 2:18

C. We increase our knowledge of God's Word. 2 Peter 1:5

D. We attend to become stronger and to grow. 1 Peter 2:2, 3

E. Attendance presents an opportunity for us to meet the Lord and be with Him. Matthew 18:20

F. Attendance guards against apostasy. 2 Peter 2:20-22; 1 Corinthians 11:30; 1 Thessalonians 5:6

G. Regular attendance is necessary because we need all the help we can get: surely something will be said or done to help us spiritually. 2 Timothy 3:16; Hebrews 4:12-15; Galatians 5:13-26; Psalms 1; 25; 46:1; 121:1, 2; 133:1

H. We should attend that we may support the truth. 1 Timothy 3:15

Why some fail to attend.

A. Fear of persecution. Matthew 10:28

B. Lack of interest. Revelation 2:4

C. Not well taught. John 6:45

D. Don't like preacher. Matthew 4:10

E. Someone mistreated them. Matthew 18:15; 2 Corinthians 11:26

F. The church not rightly run. Hebrew 13:7

G. Clothes not good enough. 1 Samuel 16:7; Matthew 6:28, 29

H. Tired; need Sunday to rest. Matthew 6:33

Conclusion: We should attend regularly and learn to enjoy it, for if we do not enjoy being with the people of God in worship here, we would not enjoy heaven even if we should go there. Our presence also will help to build up and strengthen the church. No congregation can grow without attendance. If no one attended, there would be no service; the doors would be locked, and the cause of Christ would die in that community. There are many things we may not be able to do, but we can attend if we are not ill. We can help to make a crowd. We should be present at all the services because a vacant pew has an eloquent tongue which preaches a sermon of defeat. The real reason that some do not attend faithfully and regularly the services of the church is that they have little interest in their souls and in the church. Few will admit this; usually some excuse like one of the above is given. See Luke 14:16-24.

LESSON XII: EVANGELISTS

With this study begins a close scrutiny of each of the functions of various members in the church. Probably the convert knows the evangelist best because he is "in the limelight." An elder who has "taken him under his wing," too, would be known, as would the individual who brought him to Christ, as did Andrew his brother. However, the preacher, the evangelist, being a featured member of the congregation, is probably the best-known individual to the new Christian.

Coming from the denominational world, the new member tends to place the evangelist higher than other members, for in most denominations the preacher is **the** pastor of the congregation or he is known by the title "reverend." It is of the utmost importance that one understand that in the Lord's body there is no distinction between the "lay" member and the "clergy." We have no "man of the cloth"; we are, on the contrary, all priests. The evangelist's work is specifically directed in the New Testament.

EVANGELISTS

Scriptural Text:
2 Timothy 4:1-5

Introduction: The evangelist preaches Jesus, whether the location be on a street corner, in a foreign country, via radio/television, or behind a pulpit in a local congregation.

The use of the terms meaning "a proclaimer of Good News."

A. Referring to definite work. Ephesians 4:11

B. Philip designated an Evangelist. Acts 21:8

C. Timothy urged to do the work of an Evangelist. 2 Timothy 4:5

The work of an Evangelist.

A. Philip (1) proclaimed Christ—Acts 8:5, 35; (2) was attended by miracles, confirmed the word—Acts 8:6-8 and Hebrews 2:4; (3) preached wherever opportunity afforded—Acts 8:40

B. Baptize those who believe. Acts 8:12, 38

C. "Reprove, rebuke, exhort." 2 Timothy 4:1, 2

D. Complete organization of congregations. Titus 1:5

E. Indoctrinate the church. Titus 1:13; 2:1-5

G. Give his time fully to the Lord's work. 2 Timothy 4:1-6; 1 Timothy 4:13-16; 2 Timothy 2:4, 5

H. Warn against dangers of apostasy. 1 Timothy 4:1-6

I. Protect the church from false teachers. 1 Timothy 1:3

J. Assist in building up local churches

    1. Timothy tarried at Ephesus. 1 Timothy 1:3

    2. Titus was left at Crete. Titus 1:5

K. To summarize, the work of an Evangelist was/is

1. Preach the word. 2 Timothy 4:2

2. Guard the faith. 1 Timothy 6:20, 21

3. "Handle aright the word of truth"; that is, apply it to all people and conditions as needed (2 Timothy 2:15) to the end that men might be saved.

Qualifications of an Evangelist.

A. "Keep thyself pure." 1 Timothy 5:22

B. "Gentle, apt to teach, forbearing." 2 Timothy 2:22-26

C. Diligent. 2 Timothy 2:15, 16

D. Steadfast in the faith, loyal in the truth, refusing false speculative doctrines and uncompromising toward those that teach them. 1 Timothy 6:3-11; 4:1, 6; 2 Timothy 3:14-17; 4:1-5

E. An example to them that believe. 1 Timothy 4:12

F. Careful both as to himself and what he teaches. 1 Timothy 4:16

Conclusion: Evangelists today—that is, those who undertake to spread the Gospel by publicly teaching and preaching it—should strive to fit themselves into these requirements of the New Testament as perfectly as possible. The Word of God, already confirmed, is existing now in written form that we might appeal to it for evidence that we are preaching the truth; miracles are no longer needed for that purpose. Finally, the evangelist ought to consider seriously the following verse: "Be not many of you teachers, my brethren, knowing that we shall receive heavier judgment" (James 3:1).

LESSON XIII: DEACONS; LESSON XIV: ELDERS

The officers of the church are now to be seriously considered, deacons first, then elders. The two lessons are best studied one right after the other. The new member is usually quite interested in these, the only offices designated in the New Testament. Included are the qualifications for both and the duties of both. Of significance is the member's responsibility to the elders and the respect due that office. These two have been found to be most interesting and informative studies for a new member. This hierarchy, if such it be called, is the only one sanctioned by the New Testament. What is probably most enlightening, however, is the recognition that these men are vulnerable but have acquired a maturity of faith to which any Christian man can aspire.

DEACONS

Scriptural Text:
1 Timothy 3:8-13

Introduction: The office of deacon is one of service to the church. All members do service, but the deacon is assigned a special commission by the elders of the local congregation. Every Christian should aspire to the qualifications of character outlined in the New Testament for the deacon.

Meaning of the term deacon.

A. General meaning: **Deacon** means waiter, attendant, servant (one who serves), minister. It is derived from the word **daiko**, meaning run or hasten. In this general sense of active service, it includes:

   1. Evangelists. Ephesians 6:21; Colossians 1:7; 1 Timothy 4:6

   2. Any and every faithful servant of Christ. John 12:26

B. Special meaning: From the association of the word with the office and work of bishops/elders, it is evidenced that the word **deacon** is used also in an official sense:

   1. Bishops and deacons are distinguished from the saints in general. Philippians 1:1

   2. Association of an especially qualified group with the elders indicates a regularly constituted or established office. 1 Timothy 3:8-13

Their position and work.

A. In contrast to the word **bishop** which means **overseer**, the deacon is a helper or servant of the church, working as does every other member of the congregation, under the oversight and in assistance to the bishops of the church.

B. Acts 6:1-6 gives us several insights:

   1. Deacons were selected to relieve the apostles of secular duties and responsibilities in order that they might give themselves more fully to spiritual matters.

2. These men were selected by the congregation and then appointed by the apostles.

3. The performance of the work for which they were selected constituted the full measure of special responsibility.

Their qualifications.

A. 1 Timothy 3:8-13

1. Grave (serious)

2. Not double-tongued

3. Not given to much wine.

4. Not greedy for money.

5. Holding the faith in a pure conscience.

6. Proved.

7. Husband of one wife.

8. Rules children and home well.

B. Acts 6:1-6

1. "Of honest report."

2. "Full of the Holy Spirit," bearing its fruits in his life. Galatians 5:22-24

3. "Full of wisdom."

Conclusion: In general, a deacon owes the same service to the Lord and bears the same responsibilities as does every Christian. He, however, is one to whom special responsibilities have been given. The church needs leaders who can be trusted to do the work of the church as God has laid down in His holy plan, and the leaders need to have Christian qualities and characters. Everything they do must be done in such a way that others may see their good example and follow them. In them must be found to an outstanding degree the qualities of the real Christian character.

ELDERS

Scriptural Text:
1 Timothy 3:2-7; Titus 1:6-9

Introduction: The church's organization adhered to by the New Testament churches of Christ is quite different from that which one sees in the majority of religious groups today. In the beginning, each congregation enjoyed local autonomy with elders overlooking the spiritual needs of their local church. Should we not emulate these first century Christians?

Meaning of the term elder.

A. Used to describe older age. Luke 15:25; Mark 8:31

B. Used to refer to Jewish elders of the synagogues. Matthew 16:21; Mark 8:31; Luke 9:22; Acts 4:5

C. The word **elder** names certain persons appointed to local churches to have the spiritual oversight over its members. Acts 14:23; 20:17; Titus 1:5

D. **Elder** is used the same as **bishop** and **pastor** meaning the same office and work. Ephesians 4:11; Acts 20:17; Titus 1:5-7

Responsibility and work of an elder.

A. To feed the church. Acts 20:28

B. To guard the flock from false teachers. Acts 20:29-31

C. To rule the church.

   1. With diligence. Romans 12:8

   2. As double honor. 1 Timothy 5:17

   3. Not as lords, but as examples. 1 Peter 5:3

D. To tend the flock, "exercising the oversight thereof." 1 Peter 5:2

E. To watch in "behalf of souls." Hebrews 13:17

Qualifications of an elder.

A. 1 Timothy 3:2-7
1. Without reproach.
2. Husband of one wife.
3. Temperate.
4. Sober-minded.
5. Orderly.
6. Given to hospitality.
7. Apt to teach.
8. No brawler.
9. No striker.
10. Gentle.
11. No lover of money.
12. Not contentious.
13. Ruling well his own household.
14. Not a novice.
15. Of good reputation without.

B. Titus 1:6-9
1. Blameless.
2. Husband of one wife.
3. Exhibiting self control.
4. Sober-minded.
5. Given to hospitality.
6. Able to exhort and convince the gainsayer.
7. No brawler.
8. Having children that believe, are not unruly.
9. Just, holy, a lover of good.

C. Not self-appointed, Acts 14:23, Titus 1:5

Our duty toward elders.

A. 1 Timothy 5:17, 18
B. Not to hear accusations except at mouth of two or three witnesses. 1 Timothy 5:19
C. Obey and respect them. Hebrews 13:17

Conclusion: The elders of the congregation have an awesome responsibility. They must not only see to the spiritual necessities of themselves and their families, but of all the families holding local memberships. The elder must not be a novice, therefore, but one who holds insights into God's Word as the result of deep and thoughtful study so that he can guide the work of the Lord through the membership. He must be one who can rule without being resented for that rule by his conduct. He works with other elders in the congregation and is not to assume superiority over them. His reward, if he has performed his task well, is accounted "double honor." Because of the gravity of his task, we are charged to receive not an accusation against him "except at the mouth of two or three witnesses" (1 Timothy 5:19).

LESSON XV: PERSONAL TEACHING

After becoming a Christian, one wants to tell everyone what he has found, but perhaps he feels that he does not know enough to explain. He only knows that **he** understands why. When pressed to give answers, he feels inept, though this, obviously, is not always the case. One should, at this point in the studies and after fifteen weeks of serious consideration of the Scriptures, begin feeling more secure in his faith. Teaching others is a duty, but if one has concern for those who do not have what he has—a Savior—he will take any opportunity to share that Savior's love for man. Every Christian ought to be reminded of how he was brought to Christ and of the joy he felt.

PERSONAL TEACHING

Scriptural Text:
Matthew 28:18-20

Introduction: All Christians are obligated by divine authority to teach the Bible. The Apostles were to teach the baptized all things Jesus had taught the Apostles; one thing Jesus taught was to teach the Gospel. Hence, the command to teach others is enjoined upon each baptized person today. In Hebrews 5:12 Paul says "ye ought to be teachers." Paul again said, "Woe is unto me if I preach not the gospel" (1 Corinthians 9:16). Christ said "go," and Paul said "woe" if we do not; so it is either "go" or "woe."

The duty to teach and win souls grows out of the second great commandment (Matthew 22:39). Obedience to this command will make personal evangelists out of us all. The "Golden Rule" (Matthew 7:12) will stimulate us to the same service.

We must learn that we have been saved to serve, and that we must win others to save ourselves (Ezekiel 33:8, 9). This is a fearful thought, but the wise do something about it (Proverbs 11:30).

Personal work and teaching of Jesus.

A. He did much personal work and teaching.

    1. Peter and Andrew. Matthew 4:18, 19

    2. James and John. Matthew 4:21, 22

    3. Matthew. Matthew 9:9

B. Some of Christ's most familiar sermons were preached to single hearers.

    1. New birth. John 3:1-13

    2. Living water. John 4:5-26

Personal teaching of early disciples.

A. Andrew. John 1:41, 42

B. Philip. John 1:45

C. Persecuted Christians. Acts 8:1-5

D. Personal teaching was so important that the angel of the Lord called Philip away from the multitudes in Jerusalem to preach to a lone Ethiopian. Acts 8:25-39

E. Paul taught publicly and from house to house. Acts 20:20

Ways and opportunities of personally teaching the Bible.

A. From house to house. Acts 20:20

    1. Philippian jailor. Acts 16:25-34

    2. Cornelius. Acts 10:25-48

    3. Zaccheus. Luke 19:1-10

B. By inviting them into our homes, as Matthew invited publicans and sinners into his home to dine with Jesus. Matthew 9:9, 10

C. Call those in error aside and teach them. Acts 18:24-26

D. Teach those with whom we work.

E. By godly, upright living. Matthew 6:33; Romans 12:1, 2; 2 Corinthians 6:17, 18; James 4:4; 2 Peter 1:3-11

Reasons why some are not teachers.

A. Over-cautious or fearful of saying the wrong thing. Ecclesiastes 11:4. The person who is anxious to win souls rather than just win arguments need not worry about offending reasonable people; his humility, sincerity and love for souls will nearly always make a good impression. 1 Peter 3:1

B. Some do not teach because they realize they do not know enough about the Bible to do so. Whose fault is this? We must study. 2 Timothy 2:15. We must add knowledge to faith. 2 Peter 1:5, 6

Conclusion: Had we not a direct command from Christ, we would still know to teach the good news of Jesus' death, resurrection and second coming by the examples of Christ and His disciples. However, we have been given a direct command and to withhold from others the beautiful love of Jesus is unthinkable. Our hearts should be brimming over with the desire to tell others about God's love. Through study, we can become the teacher rather than the one being taught. See Hebrews 5:12.

LESSON XVI: MUSIC IN THE WORSHIP

When one first visits a church of Christ, he is struck by the lack of instrumental music. Often this is an individual's first question regarding the church: "Why don't you use musical instruments?" The answer to that question is not nearly so important as others directly pertaining to one's soul. Suffice it to say, though, that no mechanical device can compare to the **a cappella** singing of voices united in praise to God, the creator of the human voice. Surely God knew that the blending of human voices was vastly superior to an organ or other instrument of man's design and creation. Were it not a command, the human voice lifted in song to Him would still be the greatest praise for its creator.

MUSIC IN THE WORSHIP

Scriptural Text:
Ephesians 5:19; Colossians 3:16

Introduction: Music has its place and purpose in the worship of the church. This place and purpose has been created by divine authority. In that place and purpose we must recognize the importance of (1) the kind of music authorized, (2) the purpose music serves, and (3) the manner in which it is rendered.

The kind of music specified.

A. New Testament Scriptures authorize singing only.

    1. Matthew 26:30

    2. Acts 16:25

    3. Romans 15:9

    4. 1 Corinthians 14:15

    5. Ephesians 5:19

    6. Colossians 3:16

    7. James 5:13

B. There exist only two kinds of music: vocal and instrumental. The command to sing is specific and excludes the other kind.

    1. Examples of specifics:

        (a) Genesis 6:14—gopher wood—specific.

        (b) Leviticus 16—two he goats and a ram as atonement sacrifices—specific.

        (c) Every New Testament reference is specific in that the music is vocal, excluding instrumental.

    2. When something more is done than "sing," God has been disobeyed, 2 John 9-11; 1 Corinthians 4:6

3. The New Testament Scriptures are all sufficient on this point as on all others pertaining to Christian worship and service. 2 Peter 1:2, 3; Matthew 17:5, 6; Acts 3:22, 23; 2 Timothy 3:16, 17

The purpose of singing.

A. Praises and thanksgiving unto God. Hebrew 13:15; Acts 16:25; Romans 15:9; James 5:13

B. Teaching and admonishing one another. Ephesians 5:19; Colossians 3:16
Music in Christian worship is to instruct, communicate ideas from one to another and admonish those engaged in it to right living, in addition to being a medium of praise, thanksgiving and supplication to God.

Manner of rendition.

A. "Unto God...." directed as praise to God and not for entertainment. Music in worship must not degenerate into an effort to entertain; we are singing to please God, not the multitude. Acts 16:25; Romans 15:9; Ephesians 5:19; Colossians 3:16

B. "In Spirit...." 1 Corinthians 14:15; with the heart—Ephesians 5:19. From these Scriptures, we learn that our hearts must accompany our singing and be in accord with the sentiment of the song being sung. It must be done in sincerity.

C. 'With the understanding"—1 Corinthians 14:15; one can hardly sing sincerely what he does not understand. We need to study the sentiment of the song and be sure that it is scriptural and that we understand its meaning, in order to make that meaning the sentiment of our hearts.

D. "So as to be understood...." Ephesians 5:19; Colossians 3:16; **psalms** and **hymns** appear to have been used interchangeably and not only to convey the character in general of the songs to be sung, but in particular that such compositions are to be "spiritual."

Conclusion: Nowhere in the New Testament, Christ's new covenant with all man (Hebrews 8:6), is there mention of a man-made instrument to be used in singing praises to God. The one instrument which **is** mentioned is the **heart**. It is unnecessary to add any other. Indeed, it is dangerous to do so, considering the consequences of disobeying God. Yet, why do some insist on doing that? Let us follow God's law.

LESSON XVII: THE MARRIAGE RELATIONSHIP

Usually this lesson is reserved to be the last in the series because we have dealt mostly with couples already in a happily married state. On one occasion, by request, it was covered first because the young man newly baptized and the young woman were soon to be married; they wished to know God's teachings on marriage. To the older married couple, it could be the first time they have looked at their relationship in true perspective. Nothing is more beautiful than the family in worship. Nothing can hold the family together better than a common, true faith in God. Honoring this law is the key to a successful marriage. The duties of husband, wife, father, and mother necessitate careful study. If the home provides a solid Christian foundation for the child, the child will also follow Christ, his family will worship God, and the cycle will continue, God's Word prevailing.

THE MARRIAGE RELATIONSHIP

Scriptural Text:
Genesis 2:18; Hebrews 13:4

Introduction: Marriage is the union of two lives, the cementing together of two personalities. The two hearts and lives are bound together by the strong cord of mutual love.

Ordained of God.

A. Not good for man to be alone. Genesis 2:18; Proverbs 18:22; Proverbs 19:14

B. Woman created for man. Genesis 2:18; 1 Corinthians 11:9

C. Help meet for man. Genesis 2:18

D. The first marriage. Genesis 2:21-24

The relationship.

A. One flesh. Genesis 2:24

B. Union compared to that of Christ and the church. Ephesians 5:22-23

C. Superior to parental relationship. Ephesians 5:31

D. Joined together by God. Matthew 19:6

E. Union is honorable. Hebrews 13:4

Obligations enjoined.

A. Husband to wife:

    1. To love. Ephesians 5:25-33

    2. To honor. 1 Peter 3:7

    3. Be not bitter against her. Colossians 3:19

B. Wife to husband:

1. To love. Titus 2:4

2. To be in subjection. Ephesians 5:22-24; Colossians 3:18; 1 Peter 3:1, 2

3. To respect (fear). Ephesians 5:33

The purpose of marriage.

A. For companionship. Genesis 2:18

B. For procreation. Genesis 1:28

C. To avoid fornication. 1 Corinthians 7:2

How can this relationship be dissolved?

A. By death. Romans 7:1-4

B. By fornicaton. Matthew 5:32; Matthew 19:7-9; Mark 10:10-12

1. Divorce:

   (a) One husband, one wife.

   (b) Marriage is until "death do us part."

   (c) "What therefore God hath joined together, let not man put asunder." Matthew 19:6

   (d) Only one crime for which husband and wife may be divorced— Matthew 19:9

   (e) Differences may arise, but the man and wife ought to adjust (reconcile).

"Mixed" marriages.

A. It is true that in the Patriarchal age God forbade his people marrying with heathen. Deuteronomy 7:1-3. In the days of Ezra the people were called upon to abandon their mixed marriages. Ezra 9, 10. However, this related to the preservation of a definite people unto the coming of Christ.

B. Some specific examples of Israelites marrying non-Israelites without God's disapproval or judgment:

   1. Moses married a Midianite. Exodus 2:21

   2. Ruth, ancestor of Jesus, was a Moabite. Ruth 1

C. Law of Moses even made regulation relative to an Israelite marrying a non-Israelite under certain conditions. Deuteronomy 21:10-13

   This observation is made, not to encourage Christians to marry non-Christians, but to emphasize the fact that it is an individual matter rather than an implicit law. However, such a marriage involves a tremendous risk.

Conclusion: Let us recognize and honor God's laws pertaining to marriage. Let all parents teach their children; and young people, learn and honor God's law.

NOTES

NOTES

NOTES